Baby Shower For

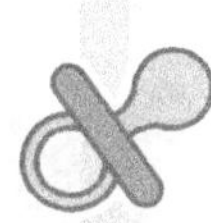

Guest Name

____

Relationship to Parents

____

Advice for Parents

____

____

____

____

Wishes for Baby

____

____

____

Guest Name

Relationship to Parents

Advice for Parents

Wishes for Baby

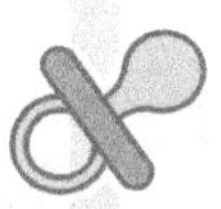

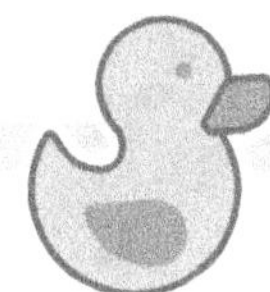

Guest Name

Relationship to Parents

Advice for Parents

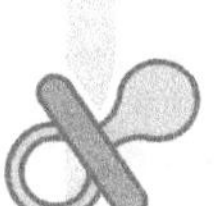

Wishes for Baby

Guest Name

Relationship to Parents

Advice for Parents

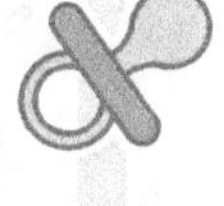

Wishes for Baby

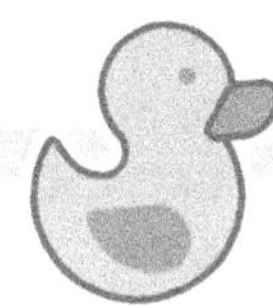

Guest Name

Relationship to Parents

Advice for Parents

Wishes for Baby

Guest Name

Relationship to Parents

Advice for Parents

Wishes for Baby

Guest Name

____

Relationship to Parents

____

Advice for Parents

____

____

____

Wishes for Baby

____

____

____

Guest Name

Relationship to Parents

Advice for Parents

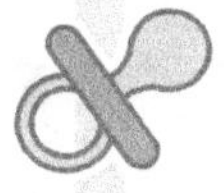

Wishes for Baby

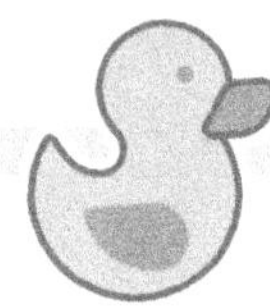

Guest Name

Relationship to Parents

Advice for Parents

Wishes for Baby

Guest Name

Relationship to Parents

Advice for Parents

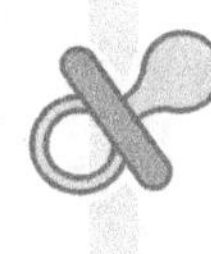

Wishes for Baby

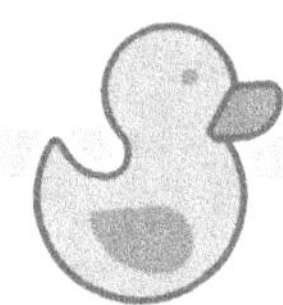

Guest Name

Relationship to Parents

Advice for Parents

Wishes for Baby

Guest Name

Relationship to Parents

Advice for Parents

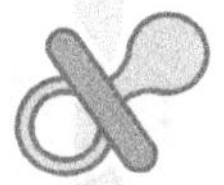

Wishes for Baby

Guest Name

Relationship to Parents

Advice for Parents

Wishes for Baby

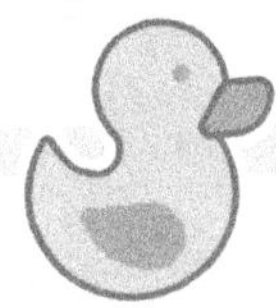

Guest Name

____

Relationship to Parents

____

Advice for Parents

____

____

____

Wishes for Baby

____

____

____

Guest Name

____

Relationship to Parents

____

Advice for Parents

____

____

____

____

Wishes for Baby

____

____

____

____

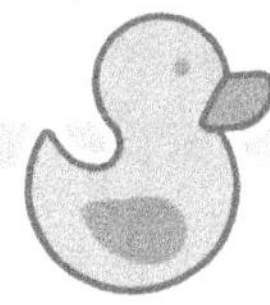

Guest Name

Relationship to Parents

Advice for Parents

Wishes for Baby

Guest Name

Relationship to Parents

Advice for Parents

Wishes for Baby

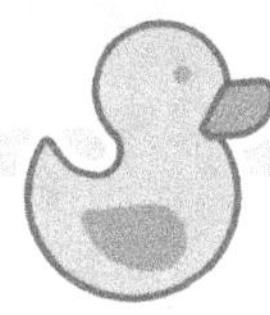

Guest Name

Relationship to Parents

Advice for Parents

Wishes for Baby

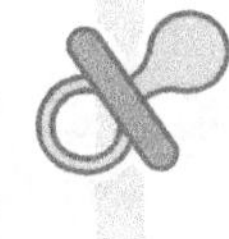

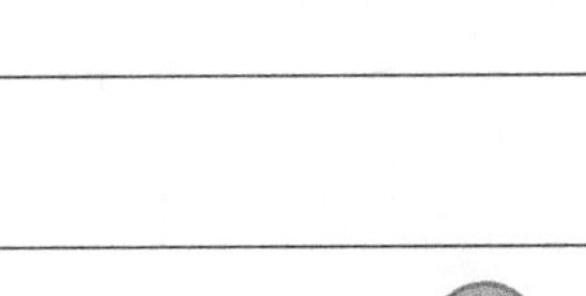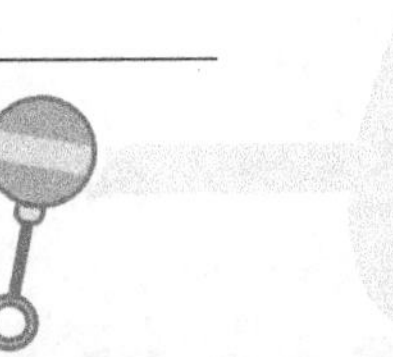

Guest Name

____

Relationship to Parents

____

Advice for Parents

____

____

____

Wishes for Baby

____

____

____

Guest Name

____

Relationship to Parents

____

Advice for Parents

____

____

____

____

Wishes for Baby

____

____

____

____

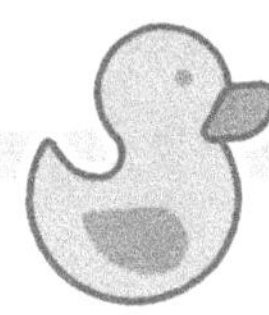

Guest Name

____

Relationship to Parents

____

Advice for Parents

____

____

____

____

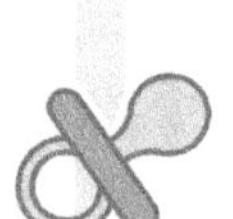

Wishes for Baby

____

____

____

____

Guest Name

Relationship to Parents

Advice for Parents

Wishes for Baby

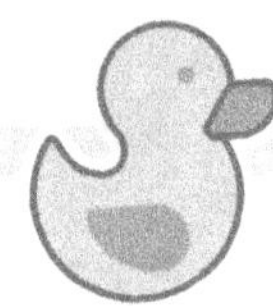

Guest Name

____

Relationship to Parents

____

Advice for Parents

____

____

____

Wishes for Baby

____

____

____

Guest Name

Relationship to Parents

Advice for Parents

Wishes for Baby

Guest Name

Relationship to Parents

Advice for Parents

Wishes for Baby

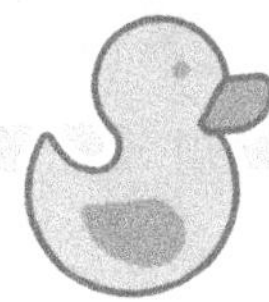

Guest Name

____

Relationship to Parents

____

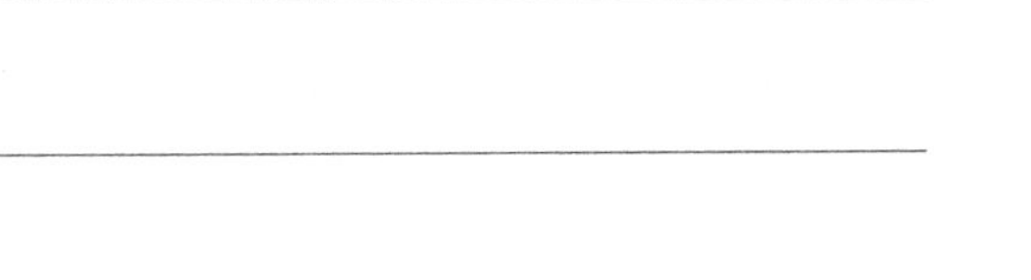

Advice for Parents

____

____

____

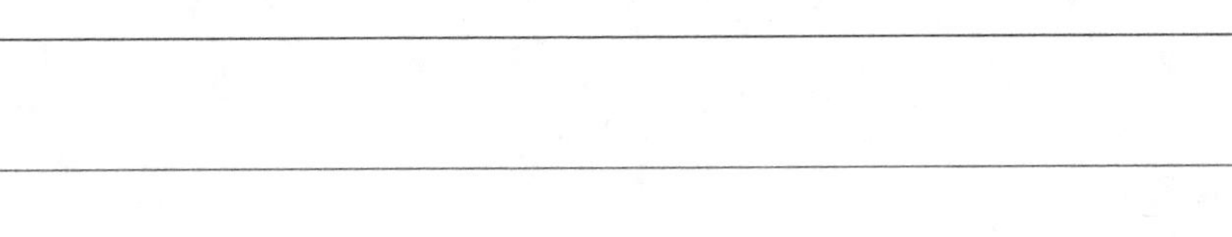

Wishes for Baby

____

____

____

Guest Name

Relationship to Parents

Advice for Parents

Wishes for Baby

Guest Name

____

Relationship to Parents

____

Advice for Parents

____

____

____

Wishes for Baby

____

____

____

____

Guest Name

____

Relationship to Parents

____

Advice for Parents

____

____

____

____

Wishes for Baby

____

____

____

____

Guest Name

____

Relationship to Parents

____

Advice for Parents

____

____

____

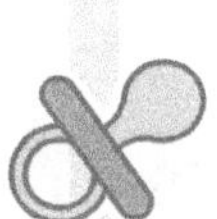

Wishes for Baby

____

____

____

Guest Name

___

Relationship to Parents

___

Advice for Parents

___

___

___

___

Wishes for Baby

___

___

___

___

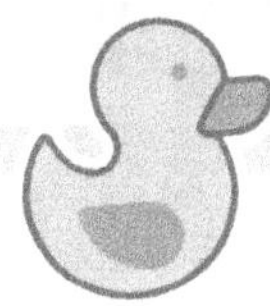

Guest Name

Relationship to Parents

Advice for Parents

Wishes for Baby

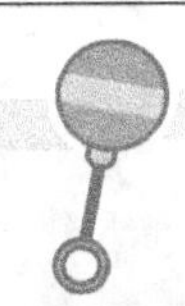

Guest Name

Relationship to Parents

Advice for Parents

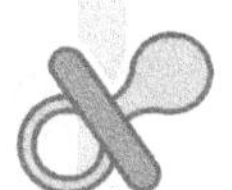

Wishes for Baby

Guest Name

Relationship to Parents

Advice for Parents

Wishes for Baby

Guest Name

____

Relationship to Parents

____

Advice for Parents

____

____

____

____

Wishes for Baby

____

____

____

____

Guest Name

____

Relationship to Parents

____

Advice for Parents

____

____

____

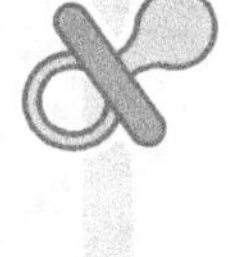

Wishes for Baby

____

____

____

Guest Name

Relationship to Parents

Advice for Parents

Wishes for Baby

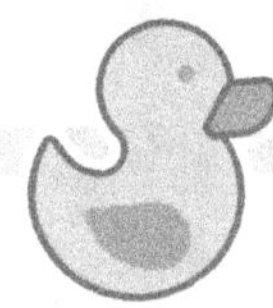

Guest Name

____

Relationship to Parents

____

Advice for Parents

____

____

____

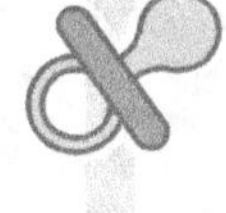

Wishes for Baby

____

____

____

____

Guest Name

____

Relationship to Parents

____

Advice for Parents

____

____

____

Wishes for Baby

____

____

____

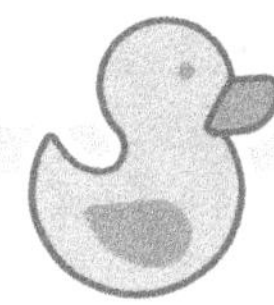

Guest Name

____

Relationship to Parents

____

Advice for Parents

____

____

____

____

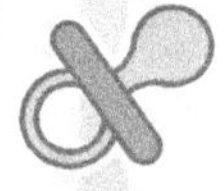

Wishes for Baby

____

____

____

____

Guest Name

____

Relationship to Parents

____

Advice for Parents

____

____

____

____

Wishes for Baby

____

____

____

____

Guest Name

Relationship to Parents

Advice for Parents

Wishes for Baby

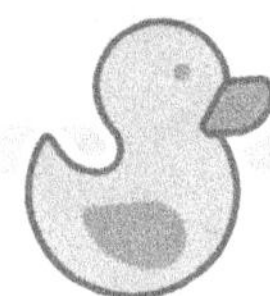

Guest Name

Relationship to Parents

Advice for Parents

Wishes for Baby

Guest Name

____

Relationship to Parents

____

Advice for Parents

____

____

____

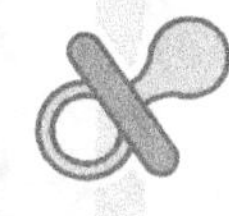

Wishes for Baby

____

____

____

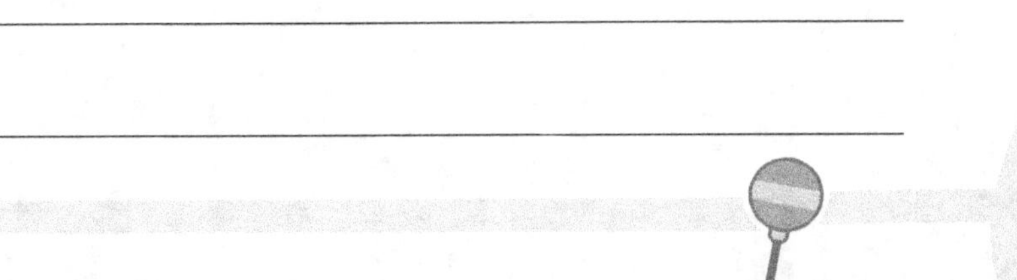

Guest Name

____

Relationship to Parents

____

Advice for Parents

____

____

____

Wishes for Baby

____

____

____

____

Guest Name

Relationship to Parents

Advice for Parents

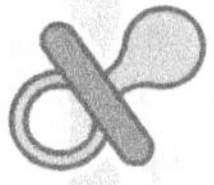

Wishes for Baby

Guest Name

Relationship to Parents

Advice for Parents

Wishes for Baby

Guest Name

Relationship to Parents

Advice for Parents

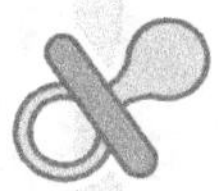

Wishes for Baby

Guest Name

Relationship to Parents

Advice for Parents

Wishes for Baby

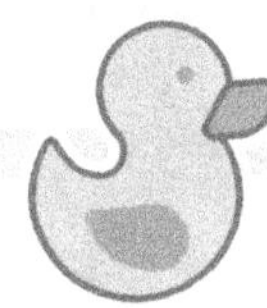

Guest Name

____

Relationship to Parents

____

Advice for Parents

____

____

____

Wishes for Baby

____

____

____

Guest Name

Relationship to Parents

Advice for Parents

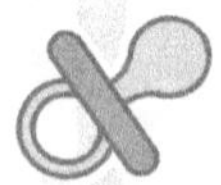

Wishes for Baby

Guest Name

Relationship to Parents

Advice for Parents

Wishes for Baby

Guest Name

____

Relationship to Parents

____

Advice for Parents

____

____

____

____

Wishes for Baby

____

____

____

____

Guest Name

Relationship to Parents

Advice for Parents

Wishes for Baby

Guest Name

Relationship to Parents

Advice for Parents

Wishes for Baby

Guest Name

Relationship to Parents

Advice for Parents

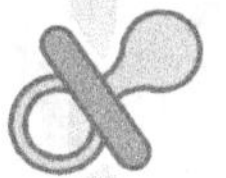

Wishes for Baby

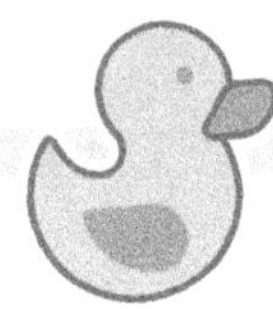

Guest Name

Relationship to Parents

Advice for Parents

Wishes for Baby

Guest Name

Relationship to Parents

Advice for Parents

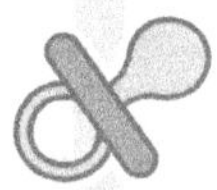

Wishes for Baby

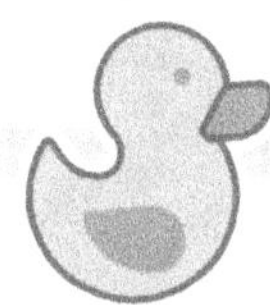

Guest Name

Relationship to Parents

Advice for Parents

Wishes for Baby

Guest Name

Relationship to Parents

Advice for Parents

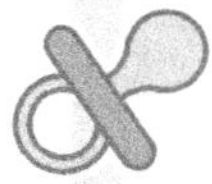

Wishes for Baby

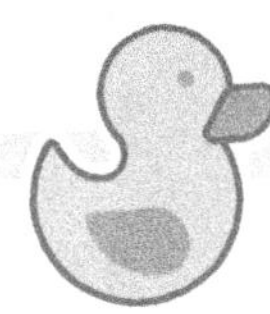

Guest Name

Relationship to Parents

Advice for Parents

Wishes for Baby

Guest Name

____

Relationship to Parents

____

Advice for Parents

____

____

____

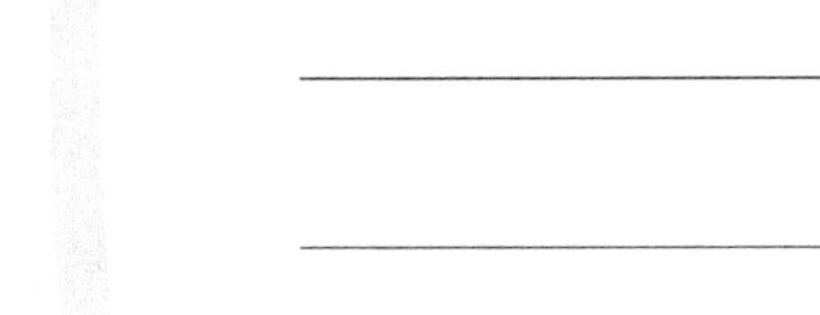

Wishes for Baby

____

____

____

Guest Name

Relationship to Parents

Advice for Parents

Wishes for Baby

Guest Name

Relationship to Parents

Advice for Parents

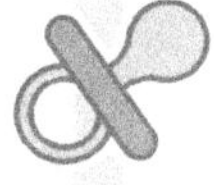

Wishes for Baby

Guest Name

Relationship to Parents

Advice for Parents

Wishes for Baby

Guest Name

Relationship to Parents

Advice for Parents

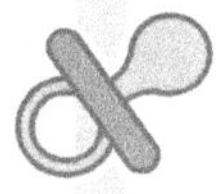

Wishes for Baby

Guest Name

____

Relationship to Parents

____

Advice for Parents

____

____

____

Wishes for Baby

____

____

____

Guest Name

Relationship to Parents

Advice for Parents

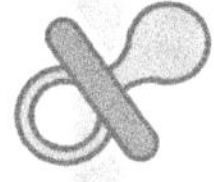

Wishes for Baby

Guest Name

____

Relationship to Parents

____

Advice for Parents

____

____

____

____

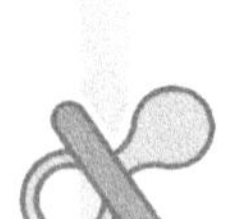

Wishes for Baby

____

____

____

____

Guest Name

Relationship to Parents

Advice for Parents

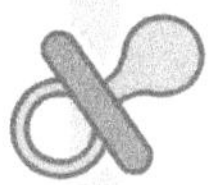

Wishes for Baby

Guest Name

Relationship to Parents

Advice for Parents

Wishes for Baby

Guest Name

Relationship to Parents

Advice for Parents

Wishes for Baby

Guest Name

Relationship to Parents

Advice for Parents

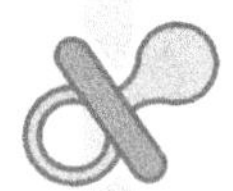

Wishes for Baby

Guest Name

Relationship to Parents

Advice for Parents

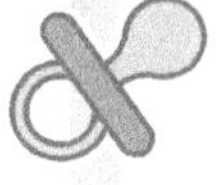

Wishes for Baby

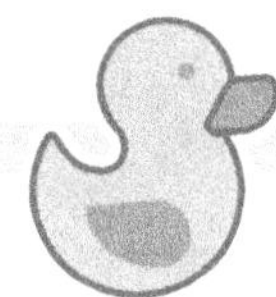

Guest Name

____

Relationship to Parents

____

Advice for Parents

____

____

____

Wishes for Baby

____

____

____

Guest Name

Relationship to Parents

Advice for Parents

Wishes for Baby

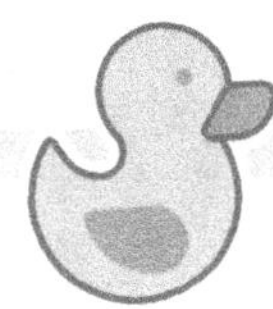

Guest Name

Relationship to Parents

Advice for Parents

Wishes for Baby

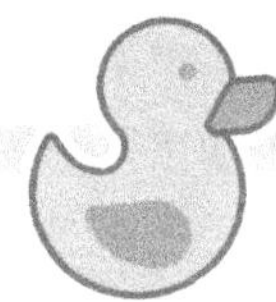

Guest Name

____

Relationship to Parents

____

Advice for Parents

____

____

____

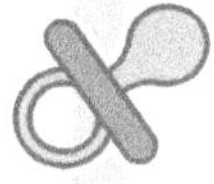

Wishes for Baby

____

____

____

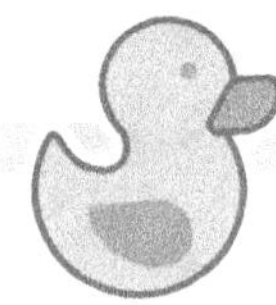

Guest Name

Relationship to Parents

Advice for Parents

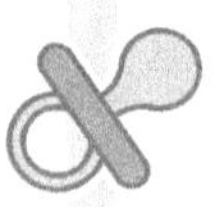

Wishes for Baby

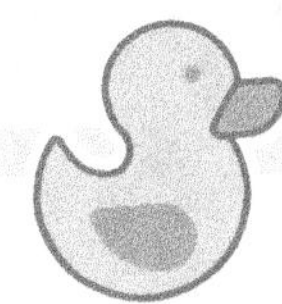

Guest Name

Relationship to Parents

Advice for Parents

Wishes for Baby

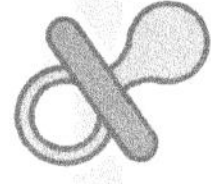

Guest Name

Relationship to Parents

Advice for Parents

Wishes for Baby

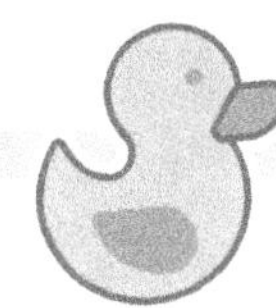

Guest Name

Relationship to Parents

Advice for Parents

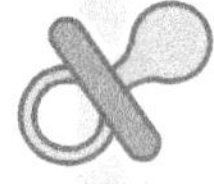

Wishes for Baby

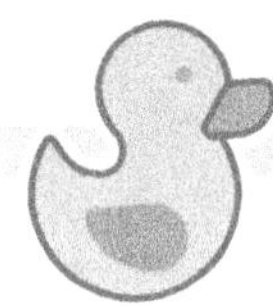

Guest Name

____

Relationship to Parents

____

Advice for Parents

____

____

____

Wishes for Baby

____

____

____

Guest Name

____

Relationship to Parents

____

Advice for Parents

____

____

____

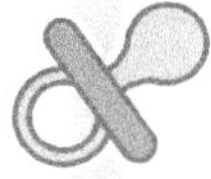

Wishes for Baby

____

____

____

Guest Name

Relationship to Parents

Advice for Parents

Wishes for Baby

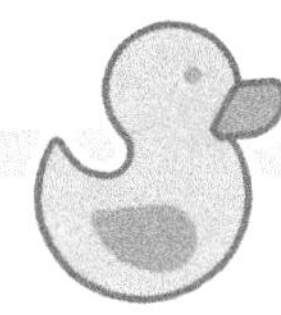

Guest Name

Relationship to Parents

Advice for Parents

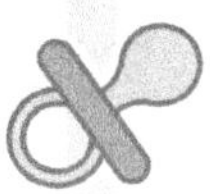

Wishes for Baby

Guest Name

____

Relationship to Parents

____

Advice for Parents

____

____

____

Wishes for Baby

____

____

____

Guest Name

Relationship to Parents

Advice for Parents

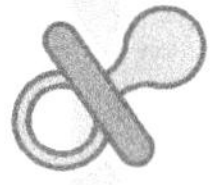

Wishes for Baby

Guest Name

____

Relationship to Parents

____

Advice for Parents

____

____

____

____

Wishes for Baby

____

____

____

____

Guest Name

____

Relationship to Parents

____

Advice for Parents

____

____

____

Wishes for Baby

____

____

____

Guest Name

Relationship to Parents

Advice for Parents

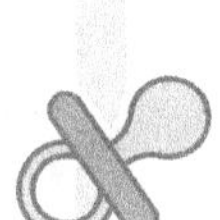

Wishes for Baby

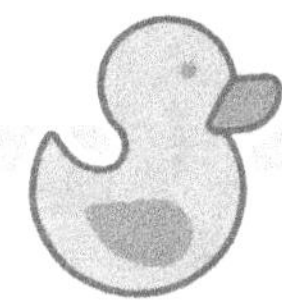

Guest Name

Relationship to Parents

Advice for Parents

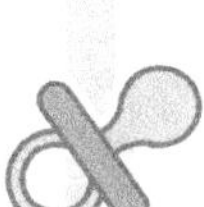

Wishes for Baby

Guest Name

____

Relationship to Parents

____

Advice for Parents

____

____

____

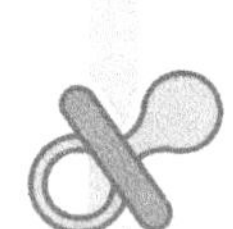

Wishes for Baby

____

____

____

Guest Name

____

Relationship to Parents

____

Advice for Parents

____

____

____

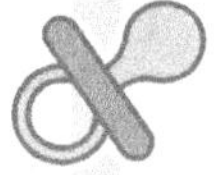

Wishes for Baby

____

____

____

Guest Name

____

Relationship to Parents

____

Advice for Parents

____

____

____

Wishes for Baby

____

____

____

Guest Name

Relationship to Parents

Advice for Parents

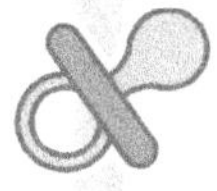

Wishes for Baby

Guest Name

Relationship to Parents

Advice for Parents

Wishes for Baby

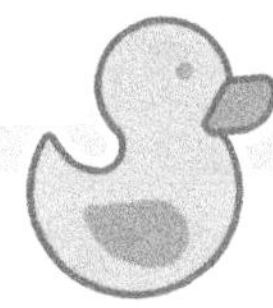

Guest Name

____

Relationship to Parents

____

Advice for Parents

____

____

____

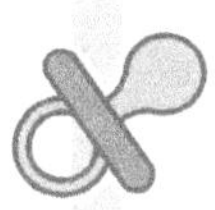

Wishes for Baby

____

____

____

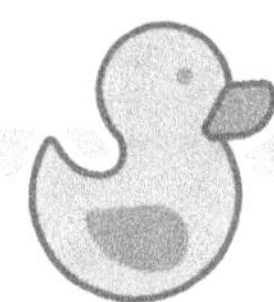

Guest Name

____

Relationship to Parents

____

Advice for Parents

____

____

____

Wishes for Baby

____

____

____

Notes / Photos

Notes / Photos

Notes / Photos

Notes / Photos

Notes / Photos

Notes / Photos

Notes / Photos

Notes / Photos

Notes / Photos

Gifts Log

Name/Email/Phone   Gift

Gifts Log

Name/Email/Phone	*Gift*

Gifts Log

Name/Email/Phone	Gift

Gifts Log

Name/Email/Phone	Gift

Gifts Log

Name/Email/Phone	Gift

Gifts Log

Name/Email/Phone	Gift

Gifts Log

Name/Email/Phone	Gift

Gifts Log

Name/Email/Phone	Gift

Gifts Log

Name/Email/Phone

Gift

Gifts Log

Name/Email/Phone   Gift